First paperback edition February 2023

Book design & Photography by Laura Clark

ISBN 979-8-9877641-0-7 (paperback)
ISBN 979-8-9877641-1-4 (hardcover)
ISBN 979-8-9877641-2-1 (ebook)

Library of Congress Control Number: 2023902838

Mountainside Bakery
Conifer, CO
www.mountainsidebakery.com

TABLE OF CONTENTS

INTRODUCTION

Hi! My name is Laura and I am a self taught baker. My sweet tooth and love for sharing my creations with others fueled my interest in baking. I also like to "experiment" in the kitchen, especially since in a previous job I was in a research & development lab. I enjoy being able to make my own food with organic ingredients that don't have any unnecessary additives, dyes, etc.

I grew up in Massachusetts just above sea level and thought I had gotten pretty good at baking by the end of college. Then I moved to Colorado where I was at 7,500ft and realized that there were different baking rules at high altitude! I struggled at first, for example my banana bread recipe that I had used for years was now coming out dry and burnt!! After some research I was finally able to learn how to adapt to baking at high-altitude. I felt comfortable for a while, however, after giving birth to my second child I was thrown another curve ball. He was very sensitive to foods and I was told to cut out dairy, gluten, soy, and cane sugar from his diet. I had never ventured into gluten free baking before, and I also had to figure out how to make things sweet without using cane sugar. Since then I have tried many different recipes, some of which were major failures and others were successes.

In the past, I have been asked by friends to make birthday, wedding, and other special occasion cakes. I decided to try to start a business and give people in the area an organic and dye free option. Then life and COVID hit, and I decided to start a blog as well. I am currently on a "mountainside" baking at about 8,600 ft, and that is how Mountainside Bakery started.

I am so glad that I have this opportunity to share my best cake recipes with you! These recipes have been made many times for birthdays, holidays, and other special occasions. I hope you enjoy them as much as I do and that you are inspired to start baking!

MENTAL INGREDIENTS FOR SUCCESSFUL BAKING

Mindset

The first thing you have to do is get into the right mindset! Have you ever noticed how when you don't want to do something or are in a bad mood that things don't go well? The same applies for baking. If you go into it thinking that you don't want to do it or are upset, then things are not going to go well. Tell yourself that you can do this and it can be fun!

Attire

You are going to have a much better time baking if you are wearing comfortable clothes that you wouldn't mind if something got on them. Baking can be very messy and I have stained a decent amount of shirts. You can also wear an apron to protect your clothes. Whatever you choose, wear something you won't be worrying about the whole time!

Environment

Make your kitchen an environment that you want to be in. Make sure you have space on the counters to work. And if possible, organize your cabinets so everything is close by and allow you to work with ease. You want to make things easier for yourself! Having the proper equipment will help with that as well. If you have kids, plan an activity to try to entertain them while you are baking. Lastly, turn on your favorite music! It is supposed to be fun, have a kitchen party!

CAKE SERVING GUIDE

Round Two Layer Cakes:

Party

Wedding

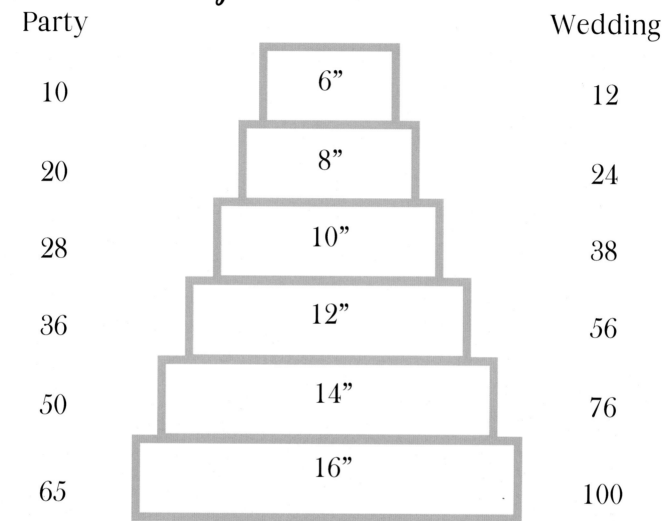

Party	Size	Wedding
10	6"	12
20	8"	24
28	10"	38
36	12"	56
50	14"	76
65	16"	100

Party Slice + 1 1/2"x 2"x 4"   Wedding Slice + 1"x 2"x 4"

Sheet Cakes:

1/4	1/2	Full
Servings: 16-20 Size: 9" x 13"	Servings: 32-40 Size: 13" x 18"	Servings: 64-85 Size: 18" x 26"

MOUNTAINSIDE Bakery

Baking Tips

BAKING TIP #1

Know Your Altitude!

Baking at High Altitude can be very frustrating, especially if you are used to baking at sea level. A lot of recipes are written for sea level and it is important to understand the adjustments that need to be made in order for recipes to come out properly. Typically you think of High Altitude baking as anything over 5,000ft above sea level, but did you know that you can start seeing effects around 3,000ft? And anything over 5,000ft is not the same, as you increase in elevation you need to keep making adjustments. I will go over some general adjustments, however, adjustments can vary depending on which recipe you are using. It is always an experiment when modifying recipes for high altitude!

Baking Powder & Baking Soda:

One of the most important things is to adjust your baking powder and baking soda in your recipes. Baked goods rise faster at altitude, so too much leavening can lead to baked goods with fallen centers. Also, baking soda is more powerful than baking powder. Once you are over about 8,500ft you might want to consider switching to just baking powder. A rough guide is below:

3,000 ft	3/4 of original amount
5,000 ft	2/3 of original amount
7,500 ft	1/2 of original amount

Once you get to about 10,000ft you might want to consider decreasing it even more.

Flour:

You want the mixture to set quicker so you need to add in some extra flour. This will make the mixture thicker and bake quicker. Once you are above 5,000ft add an extra tbsp for every cup of flour in the recipe.

Sugar:

Too much sugar can be detrimental to the structure of your baked goods. Above 3,000ft decrease by 1 1/2tsp for every cup in the recipe. Once you are over 5,000ft decrease by 1tbsp for every cup of sugar in the recipe.

Oven Temperature:

Since baked goods rise faster at high altitude, you want to set the oven temperature higher so it will set quicker. I have found that oven temperature does not change drastically with the various altitudes, I typically raise the oven temperature 10 degrees once you are over 5,000ft. If you feel that you want things to cook faster then you can raise it as much as 25 degrees above the sea level temperature, but I would not go any higher than that.

Milk:

At high altitude you want your mixture to be thicker so it can cook quicker. Because of this, you want to switch to buttermilk once you are over 3,000ft. And once you are over 5,000ft you want to add 2 tbsp of buttermilk on top of the original measurement, and add an additional 2 more tbsp for every 2,000ft after that. Example, if you are at 7,000ft you want to add 2tbsp + 2tbsp, for a total of 4 tbsp, which is 1/4cup.

Eggs:

Once you are over 5,000ft it can be helpful to add an extra egg to help add some moisture so your baked goods aren't dry. Eggs also help with the structure and texture.

Salt:

Salt is obviously used for flavor, but can also help stabilize the structure of your baked goods. Once you are over 5,000ft, you can increase the salt by 1/4-1/2 tsp. This step is optional.

As you can see there are a lot of adjustments that can be made when baking at high altitude. This can be helpful when modifying your favorite recipes. However, sometimes it is nice to find high altitude recipes where someone has gone through the trial and error and made the adjustments already! Hopefully this information has been helpful, and search around my site for recipes that are already optimized for high altitude!

BAKING TIP #2

Is it time to replace your baking powder or baking soda?

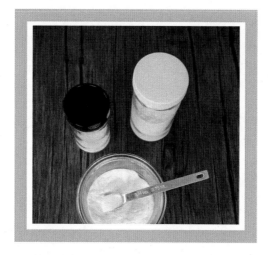

Technically baking powder or baking soda won't go "bad", however they will start to lose their potency for baking. You might find yourself having issues with your baked goods not rising as they should, which can be frustrating. That is why it is important to know if it is time to replace your baking soda or baking powder. This is especially important if you are not an avid baker, because chances are you won't use all of it before they need to be replaced. Below you can see how long each of them are supposed to last, and how to test if they need to be replaced. I like to keep track of the time by writing the date with a sharpie on the container once you open it. Or use a piece of masking tape on the bottom if you are keeping it in a glass container.

At the end there is a list of ways you can use any leftover baking powder or baking soda. There are many uses for them around the house even if they have lost their potency for baking!

When to Replace Baking Soda:

Baking soda will last for about 3-6 months in a open container (aka the box it came in) before you should replace it. If you transfer it to a closed container it could last over a year. If it is unopened it will last for several years, however not beyond the use by date on the bottom. Storing baking soda in a cool, dry place is best.

How to test if your Baking Soda needs to be replaced:

- Put a spoonful in a bowl
- Add a few drops of lemon juice or vinegar
- If it starts to fizz immediately, then it is still OK to use for baking

When to Replace Baking Powder:

Baking powder will last for about 6 months after the container is opened before it is time to be replaced. If it is unopened it will last for a few years, however, not beyond the use by date on the bottom. Storing baking powder in a cool, dry place is best.

How to test if your Baking Powder needs to be replaced:

- Put a spoonful in a bowl
- Add a little bit of hot water
- If it starts to bubble right away then it is still ok to use for baking

Don't let any extra baking soda or baking powder go to waste! After it is time to replace your baking powder or baking soda for baking, use them around the house! Below are lists of alternative uses for baking soda and baking powder.

5 Uses for Baking Soda around the house:

1. Use it as a scratch free scrub: I especially like to use this in my sinks with a scrub sponge. Sprinkle over the surface, wet the sponge, then scrub. For my kitchen sink I will add dish soap.
2. Clean and deodorize your dishwasher: Sprinkle about 1 cup in your empty dishwasher and run it on the rinse cycle.
3. Add to a load of laundry: If you add 1/2 cup to a load of laundry it can help boost the effectiveness of your detergent, brighten your clothes, eliminate odors, and balance out the pH of the water.
4. Natural nausea remedy: Add 1/2 tsp to 4 oz. warm water and drink it. This helps balance out the pH in your stomach and can help with any nausea.
5. Fire Extinguisher: For a small grease fire never use water! You can try to cover with a lid, or use baking soda instead! Just sprinkle on top or throw near the base of the flames and it could help put out the fire. However, always make sure you also have an appropriate fire extinguisher nearby in your kitchen.

5 Uses for Baking Powder around the house:

1. Use it as a scratch free scrub: Baking powder can also be used as a scratch free scrub around your house, just like baking soda
2. Clean and deodorize your carpets: Baking powder or baking soda can be sprinkled on carpets before vacuuming. This will help take out any lingering odors.
3. Add to a load of laundry: If you add 1/2 cup to a load of laundry it can help boost the effectiveness of your detergent, brighten your clothes, eliminate odors, and balance out the pH of the water.
4. Clean your microwave: Add 2 tbsp of baking powder to 2 cups of water in a microwave safe bowl. Microwave for 2 minutes, then wipe clean.
5. For grease stains: If you have a grease stain on your clothes, sprinkle some baking powder on the spot to help soak it up. After a few minutes add some dish soap and scrub gently with a wet toothbrush.

BAKING TIP #3

Check Your Oven Temperature!

You may set your oven to 350F, but is it really 350F inside? This is really important to know because ovens can vary a lot, even new ones! If it is +/- 25F or more it is going to have a big impact on your baking. You don't want to end up with burnt baked goods when you have followed the recipe exactly! That is frustrating, I have been there. Some of my previous apartment rentals have had ovens that were older than I was or were just way off, by about 50F! I of course realized this after setting off the fire alarm one time while baking something. Yes, even I have set off fire alarms while baking. It happens. The best way to prevent that is to check your oven temperature!

The easiest way to check is to get an oven thermometer. Most are under $10 and can be found almost anywhere (Amazon, Walmart, Target, etc.). Below is a good procedure to follow to check your oven temperature:

1. Place the oven thermometer in the middle of the rack that is in the middle position.

2. Check that the thermometer is reading close to your room temperature to make sure it is working properly.

3. Close your oven and set to 350F.

4. Once the oven beeps indicating that it has preheated, check the temperature. The best way would be to turn the oven light on and read the temperature without opening the oven. Once you open the oven you are going to drop the oven temperature.

5. If the temperature has still not reached 350F, wait 10 minutes and check again. Repeat 2 more times if necessary.

6. If you have waited 30 minutes past the preheat point and it is +/- more than 25F you should contact someone to have your oven calibrated, or just account for it when you are baking. For example, if you set your oven to 350F and it is only heating up to 325F, then try to set it to 375F and see if it heats up to 350F. This should be tested with the thermometer before baking anything, because ovens can be off at lower temperatures but more accurate at higher temperatures. Or you can adjust your baking times accordingly by increasing or decreasing the time it is in the oven.

If you would like, you can repeat these steps at 250F and 400F to make sure those temperatures are accurate as well. Again, sometimes an oven can be accurate at 400F but not 350F. Another thing to test would be the different rack positions. If it is not heating up to 350F in the middle position, try to lower the rack to see if you can get to 350F. If you can, then consider doing your baking on that lower rack position.

The last thing you can test for is uniformity across the rack. You can do this by moving the oven thermometer to each of the 4 corners and checking the temperature of each spot after the oven heats up to 350, but that is a little time consuming. Another way would be to get an Infrared Thermometer Gun and test different spots on your baking sheet. Place a baking sheet in the oven on the middle rack and set the oven to 350F. After the oven has preheated, wait an additional 10 minutes. Then open the oven and quickly test the temperature of the middle and 4 corners of the baking sheet to see if you find any variation. If you don't have any thermometers, you can do an old school test with cheap slices of bread.

Bread Slice Test

- Place 6 pieces of bread directly on the oven rack. Spread them out evenly so they cover the area where a baking sheet would typically be

- Turn the oven on to 350F

- Once the oven has preheated, check the bread and see if it has started to brown. If the bread has browned a lot, take them out and place on a baking sheet in the same order that they were in the oven. If not, bake an additional 10 minutes and check again

- Once the slices are out of the oven, observe if there are spots that have browned more than others. Take note of this, and you can take a picture for reference.

As you can see, when I did the test in my oven there is a small hot spot in the back center of my rack. If you do have any hot spots, you can address this by rotating your baked goods while they are cooking, or consider investing in quality baking sheets/pans that will bake more evenly. You can also make sure the oven is level. Place a level on the racks and see if you need to adjust the feet to make the oven level. A level oven can help improve uniformity. If there are still major hot spots consider having your oven calibrated. It is a good idea to check your oven temperature every year to make sure it is still working properly! If it has any issues, get it calibrated!

BAKING TIP #4

Use Baking Strips for Even Cake Layers!

When baking cake layers, I highly suggest using baking strips. Baking strips are used in order to get more even heating while baking. They are soaked in water and placed around the pan, which will prevent the edges from heating up much faster than the center of the cake. This will result in a flatter cake top, less cracking, and the edges won't be brown and dry. This is why I use baking strips for even cake layers! I feel it is especially important at high altitudes. Below you can see the difference between a cake layer that used a baking strip, and one that did not.

Baking strips are relatively inexpensive and you can find them at many big stores (Amazon, Walmart, Target, etc.). The strip is adjustable and available in a variety of sizes so you have the best fit for your cake pan. I typically use the 8 inch ones the most, which I can size down to fit a 6 inch pan as well. I have also tried a variety of brands which all seemed to work. Pick the baking strip that will work best for you.

For the best results, be sure to follow the instructions and soak them according to the directions. I try to make it my first step when baking a cake. I will get out a bowl and place all of them in there to soak while I am mixing the batter. Then they will be ready by the time you have the cake batter in the pans. After placing the strips around the pan, make sure there isn't any extra fabric hanging down that can touch the oven rack. This can cause it to discolor more and is not good for the strip. Make sure to fasten the end well or tuck in any extra fabric.

Keep in mind that the baking strip is fabric and subjected to high heat often. That means they will not last forever! I learned that the hard way. All of a sudden I was having issues with domed tops that were cracking with my normal recipe. My baking strips weren't visibly burnt or in rough shape, but they had lost their effectiveness. I replaced my baking strips, and then everything was good again! The baking strips will last for awhile, especially if you are not baking cakes all the time. But just keep in mind that it won't be forever!

I hope this information was helpful! Baking strips are an easy way to get more even cake layers. If you haven't tried them before, you will see a huge improvement with your cake layers once you start using them!

BAKING TIP #5

Use Parchment Paper to Prevent Sticking!

Having trouble with your cake sticking to the bottom of your pans? Use parchment paper to prevent sticking! It will help you get clean cake layers every time. This is especially helpful when baking larger cake layers. You don't want to go through all of that work just to have it stick! Below are instructions on how I prepare my cake pans.

How to Prepare Cake Pans:

1. Pour a little oil into the pan (I use avocado oil) and coat the inside of the pan with the oil using a paper towel.

 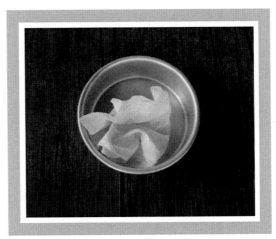

2. Sprinkle some flour into the pan and coat by shaking it around. (Best to do over the sink)

3. Take some parchment paper and keep folding in half until you have a small triangle. Hold above the cake pan with the point in the middle and measure where to cut the edge of the circle.

4. Unfold the parchment paper and make sure it fits. If it is too big just refold and trim a bit more off.

Now you are ready to place your cake batter into the pans and bake it! It is an easy extra step to use parchment paper to prevent sticking. And it will make taking your cake out of your pans a lot less stressful! Below you can see how much this helps. I baked one layer with parchment paper (right) and one without (left). There is a big difference!

You can also see that it will help you with clean up as well! Less scrubbing needed with the cake pan on the right that had the parchment paper. And parchment paper is not limited to cake pans, I also like to use it for my baking sheets as well. You can even order pre-cut parchment paper for your baking sheets, which saves time when making a lot of cookies! Basically, parchment paper can help a lot while baking, use it when you can!

HOW TO FREEZE CAKE LAYERS

Freezing cake layers in advance is a great way to fit baking a cake into your busy schedule! That way you don't have to make the cake and frost it in the same day. I find that it also helps with decorating. Below are the steps that you can take to freeze the cake layers so that they are still good when you are ready to frost the cake!

How to Freeze Cake Layers

1. Level your cake layer using a serrated knife or an adjustable cake leveler. Do this before freezing otherwise it will be very difficult to cut. Also, by doing it before freezing the crumbs will get frozen to the cake so they won't get in your frosting later.

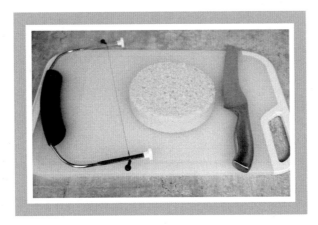

2. Get out a cake board that is the same size as your cake layer, or you can use a small cutting board. Put a layer of plastic wrap on top, and then place your cake on top of that. You want a layer of plastic wrap in between the cake and the surface otherwise it will get stuck to it. Wrap the plastic wrap around the cake.

3. Place another layer of plastic wrap on top and then wrap around the cake and the cake board. Repeat until you have 3-4 layers in total of plastic wrap.

 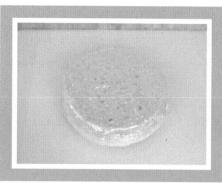 

4. Once the cake layer is wrapped, I like to take a sharpie and label what flavor it is. It is helpful if you are baking a few different layers, because they can start to look the same once they are frozen! If you want, you can add the date it as well.

5. Place the cake layer in the freezer. They will last for up to two weeks in the freezer. You can then frost the cake with them frozen or let them defrost first. Either way they will taste delicious!

Cake Recipes

VANILLA CAKE

Ingredients

	Sea Level	3,000 ft	5,000 ft	7,500 ft	10,000 ft
Oven Temp	350 °F	350 °F	360 °F	360 °F	360 °F
Eggs (Large)	4	4	5	5	5
Milk	1 cup				
Buttermilk		1 cup	1 cup plus 2 tbsp	1 1/4 cup	1 1/3 cup
Butter	1 cup	1 cup	1 cup	1 cup	1 cup
Granulated Sugar	2 cups	2 cups minus 1 tbsp	2 cups minus 2 tbsp	2 cups minus 2 tbsp	2 cups minus 2 tbsp
All-Purpose Flour	3 cups	3 cups	3 cups plus 3 tbsp	3 cups plus 3 tbsp	3 cups plus 3 tbsp
Salt	3/4 tsp	3/4 tsp	1 tsp	1 tsp	1 tsp
Baking Powder	1 tbsp	2 1/2 tsp	2 tsp	1 1/2 tsp	1 tsp
Vanilla Extract	2 tsp	2 tsp	2 tsp	2 tsp	2 tsp

Instructions

1. Preheat your oven according to the temperature in the chart above.
2. If you are using cake strips, place them in a small bowl of water to soak.
3. Crack your eggs into a small bowl and set aside.
4. Measure out your milk or buttermilk and set aside.
5. Prepare your baking pans. Use 1-2 tsp of avocado oil (or your oil of choice) to grease your pans. Then use 2-3 tbsp of flour to dust your pans.
6. Cut parchment paper to fit in the bottom of your pans and place it in the bottom.

7. In a small bowl combine the flour, salt and baking powder. Mix with a fork until they are incorporated.

8. Add the butter and sugar to your mixing bowl. Mix on medium high to high speed for a few minutes, until the mixture starts to get fluffy. Scrape the bowl and mix for another 30 seconds.

9. Add in half of the eggs and mix until just combined. Add in the rest of the eggs and mix until just combined.

10. Scrape the bowl and add in the vanilla extract. Mix until combined.

11. Add in half of the milk or buttermilk and mix until combined.

12. Add in half of the flour mixture and mix until combined.

13. Add in the rest of the milk or buttermilk and mix until combined

14. Add in the rest of the flour mixture and mix until combined.

15. Mix the batter by hand to make sure everything is incorporated. Add the batter to your cake pans. Evenly distribute the cake batter between the pans and fill until they are 1/2 to 3/4 of the way full.

16. If you are using cake strips, put those around the cake pans before putting them in the oven.

17. Baking time will vary depending on the cake size and thickness. I like to set a timer for about 35 minutes to check on how the cake is doing. I will then bake for additional time as necessary. The cake is done when a toothpick comes out clean and the sides start to pull away from the edge of the pan.

18. Take the cake out of the oven and let it cool in the pans for about 15 minutes.

19. Remove the cake from the pans and let it completely cool on a cooling rack.

20. Either frost the cake or store it in an airtight container. The cake will last for about 1 day at room temperature, or 7 days in the refrigerator. You can freeze the cake layers in plastic wrap for up to 2 weeks if you want to make them ahead of time. You could also freeze any leftover cake that has been frosted for up to 3 months in an airtight container.

CHOCOLATE CAKE

Ingredients

	Sea Level	3,000 ft	5,000 ft	7,500 ft	10,000 ft
Oven Temp	340 °F	340 °F	350 °F	350 °F	350 °F
Butter	1 cup	1 cup	1 cup	1 cup	1 cup
Water	1 1/2 cup	1 1/2 cup	1 3/4 cup	2 cups	2 cups
Cocoa Powder	1 cup	1 cup	1 cup	1 cup	1 cup
Eggs (large)	3	3	4	4	4
Granulated Sugar	2 cups	2 cups minus 1 tbsp	2 cups minus 2 tbsp	2 cups minus 2 tbsp	2 cups minus 2 tbsp
All-Purpose Flour	3 cups	3 cups	3 cups plus 3 tbsp	3 cups plus 3 tbsp	3 cups plus 3 tbsp
Salt	1/2 tsp	1/2 tsp	1/2 tsp	1/2 tsp	3/4 tsp
Baking Powder	1 tsp	3/4 tsp	2/3 tsp	1/2 tsp	1/3 tsp
Baking Soda	1 tsp	3/4 tsp	2/3 tsp	1/2 tsp	1/3 tsp
Vanilla Extract	1 1/2 tsp	1 1/2 tsp	1 1/2 tsp	1 1/2 tsp	1 1/2 tsp

Instructions

1. Preheat your oven according to the temperature in the chart above.
2. If you are using cake strips, place them in a small bowl of water to soak.
3. Crack your eggs into a small bowl and set aside.
4. In your small saucepan, add your butter and place over low heat to melt. Continue with other steps while the butter is melting. Once the butter is melted leave it on the counter for a few minutes to cool before mixing it in.

5. In your medium saucepan, add 2 cups of water. Place over high heat and bring to a boil. Remove from the heat and whisk in the cocoa powder. Set aside to cool.

6. Prepare your baking pans. Use 1-2 tsp of avocado oil (or your oil of choice) to grease your pans. Then use 2-3 tbsp of flour to dust your pans. You could also use chocolate instead of flour to make it extra chocolately.

7. Cut parchment paper to fit in the bottom of your pans and place it in the bottom.

8. In a small bowl combine the flour, salt, baking powder and baking soda. Mix with a fork until they are incorporated.

9. In your mixing bowl add the sugar.

10. Once the melted butter has cooled a bit, add it to the sugar and mix for about 30 seconds.

11. Add in half of the eggs and mix until just combined. Add in the rest of the eggs and mix until just combined.

12. Scrape the bowl and add in the vanilla extract. Mix until combined.

13. Add in half of the chocolate and water mixture. Carefully mix for a few seconds.

14. Add in half of the flour mixture and mix until combined.

15. Add in the rest of the chocolate and water mixture. Carefully mix for a few seconds.

16. Add in the rest of the flour mixture and mix until combined.

17. Mix the batter by hand quickly and then add to your cake pans. Evenly distribute the cake batter between the pans and fill until they are 1/2 to 3/4 of the way full.

18. If you are using cake strips, put those around the cake pans before putting them in the oven.

19. Baking time will vary depending on the cake size and thickness. I like to set a timer for about 30 minutes to check on how the cake is doing. I will then bake for additional time as necessary. The cake is done when a toothpick comes out clean and the sides start to pull away from the edge of the pan.

20. Take the cake out of the oven and let it cool in the pans for about 15 minutes.

21. Remove the cake from the pans and let it cool on a cooling rack.

22. Either frost the cake or store it in an airtight container. The cake will last for about 1 day at room temperature, or 7 days in the refrigerator. You can freeze the cake layers in plastic wrap for up to 2 weeks if you want to make them ahead of time. You could also freeze any leftover cake that has been frosted for up to 3 months in an airtight container.

LEMON CAKE

Ingredients

	Sea Level	3,000 ft	5,000 ft	7,500 ft	10,000 ft
Oven Temp	350 °F	350 °F	360 °F	360 °F	360 °F
Eggs (large)	4	4	5	5	5
Milk	1 cup				
Buttermilk		1 cup	1 cup plus 2 tbsp	1 1/4 cup	1 1/3 cup
Butter	1 cup	1 cup	1 cup	1 cup	1 cup
Granulated Sugar	2 cups	2 cups minus 1 tbsp	2 cups minus 2 tbsp	2 cups minus 2 tbsp	2 cups minus 2 tbsp
All-Purpose Flour	3 cups	3 cups	3 cups plus 3 tbsp	3 cups plus 3 tbsp	3 cups plus 3 tbsp
Salt	3/4 tsp	3/4 tsp	1 tsp	1 tsp	1 tsp
Baking Powder	1 tbsp	2 1/2 tsp	2 tsp	1 1/2 tsp	1 tsp
Vanilla Extract	1 tsp	1 tsp	1 tsp	1 tsp	1 tsp
Lemon Extract or Flavoring	1 1/2 tsp	1 1/2 tsp	1 1/2 tsp	1 1/2 tsp	1 1/2 tsp

Instructions

1. Preheat your oven according to the temperature in the chart above.
2. If you are using cake strips, place them in a small bowl of water to soak.
3. Crack your eggs into a small bowl and set aside.
4. Measure out your milk or buttermilk and set aside.
5. Prepare your baking pans. Use 1-2 tsp of avocado oil (or your oil of choice) to grease your pans. Then use 2-3 tbsp of flour to dust your pans.

6. Cut parchment paper to fit in the bottom of your pans and place it in the bottom.

7. In a small bowl combine the flour, salt and baking powder. Mix with a fork until they are incorporated.

8. Add the butter and sugar to your mixing bowl. Mix on medium high to high speed for a few minutes, until the mixture starts to get fluffy. Scrape the bowl and mix for another 30 seconds.

9. Add in half of the eggs and mix until just combined. Add in the rest of the eggs and mix until just combined.

10. Scrape the bowl and add in the vanilla extract and lemon extract or flavoring. Mix until combined.

11. Add in half of the milk or buttermilk and mix until combined.

12. Add in half of the flour mixture and mix until combined.

13. Add in the rest of the milk or buttermilk and mix until combined

14. Add in the rest of the flour mixture and mix until combined.

15. Mix the batter by hand to make sure everything is incorporated. Add the batter to your cake pans. Evenly distribute the cake batter between the pans and fill until they are 1/2 to 3/4 of the way full.

16. If you are using cake strips, put those around the cake pans before putting them in the oven.

17. Baking time will vary depending on the cake size and thickness. I like to set a timer for about 35 minutes to check on how the cake is doing. I will then bake for additional time as necessary. The cake is done when a toothpick comes out clean and the sides start to pull away from the edge of the pan.

18. Take the cake out of the oven and let it cool in the pans for about 15 minutes.

19. Remove the cake from the pans and let it completely cool on a cooling rack.

20. Either frost the cake or store it in an airtight container. The cake will last for about 1 day at room temperature, or 7 days in the refrigerator. You can freeze the cake layers in plastic wrap for up to 2 weeks if you want to make them ahead of time. You could also freeze any leftover cake that has been frosted for up to 3 months in an airtight container.

STRAWBERRY CAKE

Ingredients

	Sea Level	3,000 ft	5,000 ft	7,500 ft	10,000 ft
Oven Temp	340 °F	340 °F	350 °F	350 °F	350 °F
Eggs (large)	5	5	6	6	6
Milk	1/2 cup				
Buttermilk		1/2 cup	1/2 cup	1/2 cup	1/2 cup
Butter	1 cup	1 cup	1 cup	1 cup	1 cup
Granulated Sugar	2 1/4 cups	2 1/4 cups minus 1 tbsp	2 1/4 cups minus 2 tbsp	2 1/4 cups minus 2 tbsp	2 1/4 cups minus 2 tbsp
All-Purpose Flour	3 1/2 cups	3 1/2 cups	3 1/2 cups plus 3 tbsp	3 1/2 cups plus 3 tbsp	3 1/2 cups plus 3 tbsp
Salt	1 tsp	1 tsp	1 1/2 tsp	1 1/2 tsp	1 1/2 tsp
Baking Powder	1 tbsp	2 1/2 tsp	2 tsp	1 1/2 tsp	1 tsp
Vanilla Extract	1 tbsp	1 tbsp	1 tbsp	1 tbsp	1 tbsp

Strawberry Puree

	Sea Level	3,000 ft	5,000 ft	7,500 ft	10,000 ft
Fresh or Frozen Strawberries	2 cups	2 cups	2 cups	2 cups	2 cups
Lemon Juice	1/4 tsp	1/4 tsp	1/4 tsp	1/4 tsp	1/4 tsp
Granulated Sugar	1 tsp	1 tsp	1 tsp	1 tsp	1 tsp

Instructions

Strawberry Puree:

1. If using fresh strawberries, hull and slice them and place them in a small bowl. Toss them with the sugar and lemon juice and let them sit on the counter at room temperature for a few hours until juicy.

2. If you are using frozen strawberries, let them defrost and drain most of the excess liquid. Add the sugar and the lemon juice.

3. Once your strawberries are ready place them in a food processor or blender and puree. Use ¼ cup of the puree for the cake.

Strawberry Cake:

1. Preheat your oven according to the temperature in the chart above.

2. If you are using cake strips, place them in a small bowl of water to soak.

3. Crack your eggs into a small bowl and set aside.

4. Measure out your milk or buttermilk and set aside.

5. Prepare your baking pans. Use 1-2 tsp of avocado oil (or your oil of choice) to grease your pans. Then use 2-3 tbsp of flour to dust your pans.

6. Cut parchment paper to fit in the bottom of your pans and place it in the bottom.

7. In a small bowl combine the flour, salt and baking powder. Mix with a fork until they are incorporated.

8. Add the butter and sugar to your mixing bowl. Mix on medium high to high speed for a few minutes, until the mixture starts to get fluffy. Scrape the bowl and mix for another 30 seconds.

9. Add in half of the eggs and mix until just combined. Add in the rest of the eggs and mix until just combined.

10. Scrape the bowl and add in the vanilla extract and strawberry puree. Mix until combined.

11. Add in half of the flour mixture and mix until combined.

12. Add in the milk or buttermilk and mix until combined

13. Add in the rest of the flour mixture and mix until combined.

14. Mix the batter by hand to make sure everything is incorporated. Add the batter to your cake pans. Evenly distribute the cake batter between the pans and fill until they are 1/2 to 3/4 of the way full.

15. If you are using cake strips, put those around the cake pans before putting them in the oven.

16. Baking time will vary depending on the cake size and thickness. I like to set a timer for about 35 minutes to check on how the cake is doing. I will then bake for additional time as necessary. The cake is done when a toothpick comes out clean and the sides start to pull away from the edge of the pan.

17. Take the cake out of the oven and let it cool in the pans for about 15 minutes.

18. Remove the cake from the pans and let it completely cool on a cooling rack.

19. Either frost the cake or store it in an airtight container. The cake will last for about 1 day at room temperature, or 7 days in the refrigerator. You can freeze the cake layers in plastic wrap for up to 2 weeks if you want to make them ahead of time. You could also freeze any leftover cake that has been frosted for up to 3 months in an airtight container.

BANANA CAKE

Ingredients

	Sea Level	3,000 ft	5,000 ft	7,500 ft	10,000 ft
Oven Temp	340 °F	340 °F	350 °F	350 °F	350 °F
Eggs (large)	3	3	4	4	4
Milk	1/2 cup				
Buttermilk		1/2 cup	1/2 cup	1/2 cup	1/2 cup plus 1 tbsp
Medium Bananas	3	3	3	3	3
Butter	1 cup	1 cup	1 cup	1 cup	1 cup
Granulated Sugar	2 cups	2 cups minus 1 tbsp	2 cups minus 2 tbsp	2 cups minus 2 tbsp	2 cups minus 2 tbsp
All-Purpose Flour	3 cups	3 cups	3 cups plus 3 tbsp	3 cups plus 3 tbsp	3 cups plus 3 tbsp
Salt	3/4 tsp	3/4 tsp	1 tsp	1 tsp	1 tsp
Baking Powder	2 tsp	1 1/2 tsp	1 1/4 tsp	1 tsp	3/4 tsp
Cinnamon	1 tbsp	1 tbsp	1 tbsp	1 tbsp	1 tbsp
Nutmeg	1/8 tsp	1/8 tsp	1/8 tsp	1/8 tsp	1/8 tsp
Vanilla Extract	2 tsp	2 tsp	2 tsp	2 tsp	2 tsp
Chopped Walnuts (optional)	1/2 cup	1/2 cup	1/2 cup	1/2 cup	1/2 cup

Instructions

1. Preheat your oven according to the temperature in the chart above.
2. If you are using cake strips, place them in a small bowl of water to soak.
3. Crack your eggs into a small bowl and set aside.

4. Measure out your milk or buttermilk and set aside.

5. Get out your bananas. If they are frozen, defrost them in the microwave. Set them aside.

6. Prepare your baking pans. Use 1-2 tsp of avocado oil (or your oil of choice) to grease your pans. Then use 2-3 tbsp of flour to dust your pans.

7. Cut parchment paper to fit in the bottom of your pans and place it in the bottom.

8. In a small bowl combine the flour, salt, baking powder, cinnamon and nutmeg. Mix with a fork until they are incorporated.

9. Add the butter and sugar to your mixing bowl. Mix on medium high to high speed for a few minutes, until the mixture starts to get fluffy. Scrape the bowl and mix for another 30 seconds.

10. Add in half of the eggs and mix until just combined. Add in the rest of the eggs and mix until just combined.

11. Scrape the bowl and add in the vanilla extract and your bananas. Mix until combined.

12. Add in half of the flour mixture and mix until combined.

13. Add in the milk or buttermilk and mix until combined

14. Add in the rest of the flour mixture and mix until combined.

15. If you would like to use walnuts, add them in and mix until just combined.

16. Mix the batter by hand to make sure everything is incorporated. Add the batter to your cake pans. Evenly distribute the cake batter between the pans and fill until they are 1/2 to 3/4 of the way full.

17. If you are using cake strips, put those around the cake pans before putting them in the oven.

18. Baking time will vary depending on the cake size and thickness. I like to set a timer for about 35 minutes to check on how the cake is doing. I will then bake for additional time as necessary. The cake is done when a toothpick comes out clean and the sides start to pull away from the edge of the pan.

19. Take the cake out of the oven and let it cool in the pans for about 15 minutes.

20. Remove the cake from the pans and let it completely cool on a cooling rack.

21. Either frost the cake or store it in an airtight container. The cake will last for about 1 day at room temperature, or 7 days in the refrigerator. You can freeze the cake layers in plastic wrap for up to 2 weeks if you want to make them ahead of time. You could also freeze any leftover cake that has been frosted for up to 3 months in an airtight container.

CARROT CAKE

Ingredients

	Sea Level	3,000 ft	5,000 ft	7,500 ft	10,000 ft
Oven Temp	350 °F	350 °F	360 °F	360 °F	360 °F
Eggs (large)	4	4	5	5	5
Applesauce	1/2 cup	1/2 cup	1/2 cup	1/2 cup	1/2 cup
Avocado Oil	3/4 cup	3/4 cup	3/4 cup	3/4 cup	3/4 cup
Granulated Sugar	1 cup	1 cup minus 1 1/2 tsp	1 cup minus 1 tbsp	1 cup minus 1 tbsp	1 cup minus 1 tbsp
Brown Sugar	1 cup	1 cup minus 1 1/2 tsp	1 cup minus 1 tbsp	1 cup minus 1 tbsp	1 cup minus 1 tbsp
All-Purpose Flour	3 cups	3 cups	3 cups plus 3 tbsp	3 cups plus 3 tbsp	3 cups plus 3 tbsp
Salt	3/4 tsp	3/4 tsp	1 tsp	1 tsp	1 tsp
Baking Powder	1 tbsp	2 1/2 tsp	2 tsp	1 1/2 tsp	1 tsp
Baking Soda	1 tsp	3/4 tsp	1/2 tsp plus 1/8 tsp	1/2 tsp	1/4 tsp plus 1/8 tsp
Cinnamon	2 tsp	2 tsp	2 tsp	2 tsp	2 tsp
Ginger	1/2 tsp	1/2 tsp	1/2 tsp	1/2 tsp	1/2 tsp
Nutmeg	1/4 tsp	1/4 tsp	1/4 tsp	1/4 tsp	1/4 tsp
All Spice	1/4 tsp	1/4 tsp	1/4 tsp	1/4 tsp	1/4 tsp
Vanilla Extract	2 tsp	2 tsp	2 tsp	2 tsp	2 tsp
Shredded Carrots	3 cups	3 cups	3 cups	3 cups	3 cups
Chopped Walnuts	1 cup	1 cup	1 cup	1 cup	1 cup
Chopped Dates or Raisins (optional)	1/2 cup	1/2 cup	1/2 cup	1/2 cup	1/2 cup

MOUNTAINSIDE Bakery

Instructions

1. Preheat your oven according to the temperature in the chart above.

2. If you are using cake strips, place them in a small bowl of water to soak.

3. Crack your eggs into a small bowl and set aside.

4. Prepare your baking pans. Use 1-2 tsp of avocado oil (or your oil of choice) to grease your pans. Then use 2-3 tbsp of flour to dust your pans.

5. Cut parchment paper to fit in the bottom of your pans and place it in the bottom.

6. Add the applesauce, avocado oil, granulated sugar and brown sugar to your mixing bowl. Mix on medium high to high speed for a few minutes, until the mixture starts to get lighter in color. Scrape the bowl and mix for another 30 seconds.

7. In a small bowl combine the flour, salt, baking powder, baking soda, cinnamon, ginger, nutmeg and all spice. Mix with a fork until they are incorporated.

8. Add in half of the eggs and mix until just combined. Add in the rest of the eggs and mix until just combined.

9. Scrape the bowl and add in the vanilla extract. Mix until combined.

10. Add in half of the flour mixture and mix until combined.

11. Add in the rest of the flour mixture and mix until combined.

12. Add in the carrots, walnuts, and the raisins or dates if you want to add those. The raisins or dates are optional. Mix until just combined.

13. Mix the batter by hand to make sure everything is incorporated. Add the batter to your cake pans. Evenly distribute the cake batter between the pans and fill until they are 1/2 to 3/4 of the way full.

14. If you are using cake strips, put those around the cake pans before putting them in the oven.

15. Baking time will vary depending on the cake size and thickness. I like to set a timer for about 35 minutes to check on how the cake is doing. I will then bake for additional time as necessary. The cake is done when a toothpick comes out clean and the sides start to pull away from the edge of the pan.

16. Take the cake out of the oven and let it cool in the pans for about 15 minutes.

17. Remove the cake from the pans and let it completely cool on a cooling rack.

18. Either frost the cake or store it in an airtight container. The cake will last for about 1 day at room temperature, or 7 days in the refrigerator. You can freeze the cake layers in plastic wrap for up to 2 weeks if you want to make them ahead of time. You could also freeze any leftover cake that has been frosted for up to 3 months in an airtight container.

SPICE CAKE

Ingredients

	Sea Level	3,000 ft	5,000 ft	7,500 ft	10,000 ft
Oven Temp	350 °F	350 °F	360 °F	360 °F	360 °F
Eggs (large)	5	5	6	6	6
Milk	1 cup				
Buttermilk		1 cup	1 cup plus 2 tbsp	1 1/4 cup	1 1/3 cup
Butter	1 1/2 cup	1 1/2 cup	1 1/2 cup	1 1/2 cup	1 1/2 cup
Granulated Sugar	2 cups	2 cups minus 1 tbsp	2 cups minus 2 tbsp	2 cups minus 2 tbsp	2 cups minus 2 tbsp
All-Purpose Flour	3 cups	3 cups	3 cups plus 3 tbsp	3 cups plus 3 tbsp	3 cups plus 3 tbsp
Salt	3/4 tsp	3/4 tsp	1 tsp	1 tsp	1 tsp
Baking Soda	1 tsp	3/4 tsp	1/2 tsp plus 1/8 tsp	1/2 tsp	1/4 tsp plus 1/8 tsp
Cinnamon	2 tsp	2 tsp	2 tsp	2 tsp	2 tsp
Ginger	1 tsp	1 tsp	1 tsp	1 tsp	1 tsp
Nutmeg	1/2 tsp	1/2 tsp	1/2 tsp	1/2 tsp	1/2 tsp
Cloves	1/4 tsp	1/4 tsp	1/4 tsp	1/4 tsp	1/4 tsp
Vanilla Extract	1 tsp	1 tsp	1 tsp	1 tsp	1 tsp

Instructions

1. Preheat your oven according to the temperature in the chart above.
2. If you are using cake strips, place them in a small bowl of water to soak.
3. Crack your eggs into a small bowl and set aside.

4. Measure out your milk or buttermilk and set aside.

5. Prepare your baking pans. Use 1-2 tsp of avocado oil (or your oil of choice) to grease your pans. Then use 2-3 tbsp of flour to dust your pans.

6. Cut parchment paper to fit in the bottom of your pans and place it in the bottom.

7. In a small bowl combine the flour, salt, baking soda, cinnamon, ginger, nutmeg and cloves. Mix with a fork until they are incorporated.

8. Add the butter and sugar to your mixing bowl. Mix on medium high to high speed for a few minutes, until the mixture starts to get fluffy. Scrape the bowl and mix for another 30 seconds.

9. Add in half of the eggs and mix until just combined. Add in the rest of the eggs and mix until just combined.

10. Scrape the bowl and add in the vanilla extract. Mix until combined.

11. Add in half of the milk or buttermilk and mix until combined.

12. Add in half of the flour mixture and mix until combined.

13. Add in the rest of the milk or buttermilk and mix until combined

14. Add in the rest of the flour mixture and mix until combined.

15. Mix the batter by hand to make sure everything is incorporated. Add the batter to your cake pans. Evenly distribute the cake batter between the pans and fill until they are 1/2 to 3/4 of the way full.

16. If you are using cake strips, put those around the cake pans before putting them in the oven.

17. Baking time will vary depending on the cake size and thickness. I like to set a timer for about 35 minutes to check on how the cake is doing. I will then bake for additional time as necessary. The cake is done when a toothpick comes out clean and the sides start to pull away from the edge of the pan.

18. Take the cake out of the oven and let it cool in the pans for about 15 minutes.

19. Remove the cake from the pans and let it completely cool on a cooling rack.

20. Either frost the cake or store it in an airtight container. The cake will last for about 1 day at room temperature, or 7 days in the refrigerator. You can freeze the cake layers in plastic wrap for up to 2 weeks if you want to make them ahead of time. You could also freeze any leftover cake that has been frosted for up to 3 months in an airtight container.

PUMPKIN SPICE CAKE

Ingredients

	Sea Level	3,000 ft	5,000 ft	7,500 ft	10,000 ft
Oven Temp	340 °F	340 °F	350 °F	350 °F	350 °F
Eggs (large)	4	4	5	5	5
Milk	1/2 cup				
Buttermilk		1/2 cup	2/3 cup	3/4 cup	3/4 cup
Butter	1 cup	1 cup	1 cup	1 cup	1 cup
Granulated Sugar	1 1/2 cups	1 1/2 cups minus 1 tbsp	1 1/2 cups minus 2 tbsp	1 1/2 cups minus 2 tbsp	1 1/2 cups minus 2 tbsp
Brown Sugar	1/2 cup	1/2 cup	1/2 cup	1/2 cup	1/2 cup
Pumpkin Puree	1 cup	1 cup	1 cup	1 cup	1 cup
All-Purpose Flour	3 cups	3 cups	3 cups plus 3 tbsp	3 cups plus 3 tbsp	3 cups plus 3 tbsp
Salt	3/4 tsp	3/4 tsp	1 tsp	1 tsp	1 tsp
Baking Powder	1 tbsp	2 1/2 tsp	2 tsp	1 1/2 tsp	1 tsp
Vanilla Extract	1 tsp	1 tsp	1 tsp	1 tsp	1 tsp
Pumpkin Spice	1 tbsp	1 tbsp	1 tbsp	1 tbsp	1 tbsp

Instructions

1. Preheat your oven according to the temperature in the chart above.
2. If you are using cake strips, place them in a small bowl of water to soak.
3. Crack your eggs into a small bowl and set aside.
4. Measure out your milk or buttermilk and set aside.

5. Prepare your baking pans. Use 1-2 tsp of avocado oil (or your oil of choice) to grease your pans. Then use 2-3 tbsp of flour to dust your pans.

6. Cut parchment paper to fit in the bottom of your pans and place it in the bottom.

7. In a small bowl combine the flour, salt, baking powder and pumpkin spice. Mix with a fork until they are incorporated.

8. Add the butter, granulated sugar and brown sugar to your mixing bowl. Mix on medium high to high speed for a few minutes, until the mixture starts to get fluffy. Scrape the bowl and mix for another 30 seconds.

9. Add in half of the eggs and mix until just combined. Add in the rest of the eggs and mix until just combined.

10. Scrape the bowl and add in the vanilla extract and pumpkin puree. Mix until combined.

11. Add in half of the milk or buttermilk and mix until combined.

12. Add in half of the flour mixture and mix until combined.

13. Add in the rest of the milk or buttermilk and mix until combined

14. Add in the rest of the flour mixture and mix until combined.

15. Mix the batter by hand to make sure everything is incorporated. Add the batter to your cake pans. Evenly distribute the cake batter between the pans and fill until they are 1/2 to 3/4 of the way full.

16. If you are using cake strips, put those around the cake pans before putting them in the oven.

17. Baking time will vary depending on the cake size and thickness. I like to set a timer for about 35 minutes to check on how the cake is doing. I will then bake for additional time as necessary. The cake is done when a toothpick comes out clean and the sides start to pull away from the edge of the pan.

18. Take the cake out of the oven and let it cool in the pans for about 15 minutes.

19. Remove the cake from the pans and let it completely cool on a cooling rack.

20. Either frost the cake or store it in an airtight container. The cake will last for about 1 day at room temperature, or 7 days in the refrigerator. You can freeze the cake layers in plastic wrap for up to 2 weeks if you want to make them ahead of time. You could also freeze any leftover cake that has been frosted for up to 3 months in an airtight container.

LEMON RICOTTA CAKE

Ingredients

	Sea Level	3,000 ft	5,000 ft	7,500 ft	10,000 ft
Oven Temp	325 °F	325 °F	340 °F	340 °F	340 °F
Eggs (large)	3	3	4	4	4
Milk	1/2 cup				
Buttermilk		1/2 cup	2/3 cup	3/4 cup	3/4 cup plus 1 tbsp
Ricotta Cheese (whole milk)	1 cup	1 cup	1 cup	1 cup	1 cup
Butter	1 cup	1 cup	1 cup	1 cup	1 cup
Granulated Sugar	2 cups	2 cups minus 1 tbsp	2 cups minus 2 tbsp	2 cups minus 2 tbsp	2 cups minus 2 tbsp
All-Purpose Flour	3 cups	3 cups	3 cups plus 3 tbsp	3 cups plus 3 tbsp	3 cups plus 3 tbsp
Salt	3/4 tsp	3/4 tsp	1 tsp	1 tsp	1 tsp
Baking Powder	2 tsp	1 1/2 tsp	1 1/4 tsp	1 tsp	3/4 tsp
Vanilla Extract	1 1/2 tsp	1 1/2 tsp	1 1/2 tsp	1 1/2 tsp	1 1/2 tsp
Lemon Extract or Flavor (optional)	1/2 tsp	1/2 tsp	1/2 tsp	1/2 tsp	1/2 tsp

Instructions

1. Preheat your oven according to the temperature in the chart above.
2. If you are using cake strips, place them in a small bowl of water to soak.
3. Crack your eggs into a small bowl and set aside.
4. Measure out your milk or buttermilk and your ricotta cheese. Set them aside.

5. Prepare your baking pans. Use 1-2 tsp of avocado oil (or your oil of choice) to grease your pans. Then use 2-3 tbsp of flour to dust your pans.

6. Cut parchment paper to fit in the bottom of your pans and place it in the bottom.

7. In a small bowl combine the flour, salt and baking powder. Mix with a fork until they are incorporated.

8. Add the butter and sugar to your mixing bowl. Mix on medium high to high speed for a few minutes, until the mixture starts to get fluffy. Scrape the bowl and mix for another 30 seconds.

9. Add in half of the eggs and mix until just combined. Add in the rest of the eggs and mix until just combined.

10. Scrape the bowl and add in the vanilla extract and lemon extract or flavor. Mix until combined. If you don't want to add lemon extract, just add another ½ tsp of vanilla extract.

11. Add in the ricotta cheese and mix until combined.

12. Add in half of the flour mixture and mix until combined.

13. Add in the milk or buttermilk and mix until combined.

14. Add in the rest of the flour mixture and mix until combined.

15. Mix the batter by hand to make sure everything is incorporated. Add the batter to your cake pans. Evenly distribute the cake batter between the pans and fill until they are 1/2 to 3/4 of the way full.

16. If you are using cake strips, put those around the cake pans before putting them in the oven.

17. Baking time will vary depending on the cake size and thickness. I like to set a timer for about 35 minutes to check on how the cake is doing. I will then bake for additional time as necessary. The cake is done when a toothpick comes out clean and the sides start to pull away from the edge of the pan.

18. Take the cake out of the oven and let it cool in the pans for about 15 minutes.

19. Remove the cake from the pans and let it completely cool on a cooling rack.

20. Either frost the cake or store it in an airtight container. The cake will last for about 1 day at room temperature, or 7 days in the refrigerator. You can freeze the cake layers in plastic wrap for up to 2 weeks if you want to make them ahead of time. You could also freeze any leftover cake that has been frosted for up to 3 months in an airtight container.

ESPRESSO CAKE

Ingredients

	Sea Level	3,000 ft	5,000 ft	7,500 ft	10,000 ft
Oven Temp	325 °F	325 °F	340 °F	340 °F	340 °F
Eggs (large)	4	4	5	5	5
Milk	1/2 cup				
Buttermilk		1/2 cup	1/2 cup plus 2 tbsp	2/3 cup	2/3 cup plus 1 tbsp
Water (warm)	1/2 cup	1/2 cup	1/2 cup plus 1 tbsp	2/3 cup	2/3 cup
Instant Coffee	1/4 cup	1/4 cup	1/4 cup	1/4 cup	1/4 cup
Butter	1 cup	1 cup	1 cup	1 cup	1 cup
Granulated Sugar	2 cups	2 cups minus 1 tbsp	2 cups minus 2 tbsp	2 cups minus 2 tbsp	2 cups minus 2 tbsp
All-Purpose Flour	3 1/4 cups	3 1/4 cups	3 1/4 cups plus 3 tbsp	3 1/4 cups plus 3 tbsp	3 1/4 cups plus 3 tbsp
Salt	3/4 tsp	3/4 tsp	1 tsp	1 tsp	1 tsp
Baking Powder	1 tbsp	2 1/2 tsp	2 tsp	1 1/2 tsp	1 tsp
Vanilla Extract	1 1/2 tsp	1 1/2 tsp	1 1/2 tsp	1 1/2 tsp	1 1/2 tsp

Instructions

Preheat your oven according to the temperature in the chart above.

1. If you are using cake strips, place them in a small bowl of water to soak.
2. Crack your eggs into a small bowl and set aside.
3. Measure out your milk or buttermilk and set aside.

4. Measure out the water and heat it in the microwave or on the stove, then add the instant coffee to the water. Mix until it is incorporated.

5. Prepare your baking pans. Use 1-2 tsp of avocado oil (or your oil of choice) to grease your pans. Then use 2-3 tbsp of flour to dust your pans.

6. Cut parchment paper to fit in the bottom of your pans and place it in the bottom.

7. In a small bowl combine the flour, salt and baking powder. Mix with a fork until they are incorporated.

8. Add the butter and sugar to your mixing bowl. Mix on medium high to high speed for a few minutes, until the mixture starts to get fluffy. Scrape the bowl and mix for another 30 seconds.

9. Add in half of the eggs and mix until just combined. Add in the rest of the eggs and mix until just combined.

10. Scrape the bowl and add in the vanilla extract. Mix until combined.

11. Add in half of the milk or buttermilk and mix until combined.

12. Add in half of the flour mixture and mix until combined.

13. Add in the rest of the milk or buttermilk and mix until combined

14. Add in the rest of the flour mixture and mix until combined.

15. Mix the batter by hand to make sure everything is incorporated. Add the batter to your cake pans. Evenly distribute the cake batter between the pans and fill until they are 1/2 to 3/4 of the way full.

16. If you are using cake strips, put those around the cake pans before putting them in the oven.

17. Baking time will vary depending on the cake size and thickness. I like to set a timer for about 35 minutes to check on how the cake is doing. I will then bake for additional time as necessary. The cake is done when a toothpick comes out clean and the sides start to pull away from the edge of the pan.

18. Take the cake out of the oven and let it cool in the pans for about 15 minutes.

19. Remove the cake from the pans and let it completely cool on a cooling rack.

20. Either frost the cake or store it in an airtight container. The cake will last for about 1 day at room temperature, or 7 days in the refrigerator. You can freeze the cake layers in plastic wrap for up to 2 weeks if you want to make them ahead of time. You could also freeze any leftover cake that has been frosted for up to 3 months in an airtight container.

PEANUT BUTTER CAKE

Ingredients

	Sea Level	3,000 ft	5,000 ft	7,500 ft	10,000 ft
Oven Temp	340 °F	340 °F	350 °F	350 °F	350 °F
Eggs (large)	2	2	3	3	3
Milk	1 cup				
Buttermilk		1 cup	1 cup plus 2 tbsp	1 1/4 cup	1 1/3 cup
Peanut Butter (natural)	3/4 cup	3/4 cup	3/4 cup	3/4 cup	3/4 cup
Butter	1/2 cup	1/2 cup	1/2 cup	1/2 cup	1/2 cup
Granulated Sugar	2 cups	2 cups minus 1 tbsp	2 cups minus 2 tbsp	2 cups minus 2 tbsp	2 cups minus 2 tbsp
All-Purpose Flour	3 cups	3 cups	3 cups plus 3 tbsp	3 cups plus 3 tbsp	3 cups plus 3 tbsp
Salt	1 1/4 tsp	1 1/4 tsp	1 1/2 tsp	1 1/2 tsp	1 1/2 tsp
Baking Powder	1 tbsp	2 1/2 tsp	2 tsp	1 1/2 tsp	1 tsp
Vanilla Extract	1 1/2 tsp	1 1/2 tsp	1 1/2 tsp	1 1/2 tsp	1 1/2 tsp

Instructions

1. Preheat your oven according to the temperature in the chart above.
2. If you are using cake strips, place them in a small bowl of water to soak.
3. Crack your eggs into a small bowl and set aside.
4. Measure out your milk or buttermilk and peanut butter. Set them aside.
5. Prepare your baking pans. Use 1-2 tsp of avocado oil (or your oil of choice) to grease your pans. Then use 2-3 tbsp of flour to dust your pans.

6. Cut parchment paper to fit in the bottom of your pans and place it in the bottom.

7. In a small bowl combine the flour, salt and baking powder. Mix with a fork until they are incorporated.

8. Add the butter and sugar to your mixing bowl. Mix on medium high to high speed for a few minutes, until the mixture starts to get fluffy. Scrape the bowl and mix for another 30 seconds.

9. Add in half of the eggs and mix until just combined. Add in the rest of the eggs and mix until just combined.

10. Scrape the bowl and add in the vanilla extract and peanut butter. Mix until combined.

11. Add in half of the milk or buttermilk and mix until combined.

12. Add in half of the flour mixture and mix until combined.

13. Add in the rest of the milk or buttermilk and mix until combined

14. Add in the rest of the flour mixture and mix until combined.

15. Mix the batter by hand to make sure everything is incorporated. Add the batter to your cake pans. Evenly distribute the cake batter between the pans and fill until they are 1/2 to 3/4 of the way full.

16. If you are using cake strips, put those around the cake pans before putting them in the oven.

17. Baking time will vary depending on the cake size and thickness. I like to set a timer for about 35 minutes to check on how the cake is doing. I will then bake for additional time as necessary. The cake is done when a toothpick comes out clean and the sides start to pull away from the edge of the pan.

18. Take the cake out of the oven and let it cool in the pans for about 15 minutes.

19. Remove the cake from the pans and let it completely cool on a cooling rack.

20. Either frost the cake or store it in an airtight container. The cake will last for about 1 day at room temperature, or 7 days in the refrigerator. You can freeze the cake layers in plastic wrap for up to 2 weeks if you want to make them ahead of time. You could also freeze any leftover cake that has been frosted for up to 3 months in an airtight container.

RED VELVET CAKE

Ingredients

	Sea Level	3,000 ft	5,000 ft	7,500 ft	10,000 ft
Oven Temp	350 °F	350 °F	360 °F	360 °F	360 °F
Eggs (large)	3	3	4	4	4
Milk	1 cup				
Buttermilk		1 cup	1 cup plus 2 tbsp	1 1/4 cup	1 1/3 cup
Butter	1 cup	1 cup	1 cup	1 cup	1 cup
Granulated Sugar	1 1/2 cups	1 1/2 cups minus 1 1/2 tsp	1 1/2 cups minus 1 tbsp	1 1/2 cups minus 1 tbsp	1 1/2 cups minus 1 tbsp
All-Purpose Flour	3 cups	3 cups	3 cups plus 3 tbsp	3 cups plus 3 tbsp	3 cups plus 3 tbsp
Cocoa Powder	2 tbsp	2 tbsp	2 tbsp	2 tbsp	2 tbsp
Salt	3/4 tsp	3/4 tsp	1 tsp	1 tsp	1 tsp
Vanilla Extract	1 1/2 tsp	1 1/2 tsp	1 1/2 tsp	1 1/2 tsp	1 1/2 tsp
Baking Soda	1 1/2 tsp	1 1/4 tsp	1 tsp	3/4 tsp	1/2 tsp
Vinegar	1 tbsp	1 tbsp	1 tbsp	1 tbsp	1 tbsp
Red Food Coloring	1 tbsp or 1-2 packets of natural food coloring	1 tbsp or 1-2 packets of natural food coloring	1 tbsp or 1-2 packets of natural food coloring	1 tbsp or 1-2 packets of natural food coloring	1 tbsp or 1-2 packets of natural food coloring

Instructions

1. Preheat your oven according to the temperature in the chart above.
2. If you are using cake strips, place them in a small bowl of water to soak.
3. Crack your eggs into a small bowl and set aside.

4. Measure out your milk or buttermilk and set aside.

5. Prepare your baking pans. Use 1-2 tsp of avocado oil (or your oil of choice) to grease your pans. Then use 2-3 tbsp of flour to dust your pans.

6. Cut parchment paper to fit in the bottom of your pans and place it in the bottom.

7. In a small bowl combine the flour, cocoa powder and salt. Mix with a fork until they are incorporated.

8. Add the butter and sugar to your mixing bowl. Mix on medium high to high speed for a few minutes, until the mixture starts to get fluffy. Scrape the bowl and mix for another 30 seconds.

9. Add in half of the eggs and mix until just combined. Add in the rest of the eggs and mix until just combined.

10. Scrape the bowl and add in the vanilla extract and your choice of food coloring. Mix until combined.

11. Add in half of the milk or buttermilk and mix until combined.

12. Add in half of the flour mixture and mix until combined.

13. Add in the rest of the milk or buttermilk and mix until combined

14. Add in the rest of the flour mixture and mix until combined.

15. In a small bowl mix the vinegar and baking soda together. Add it to the cake batter and mix gently until it is just incorporated.

16. Mix the batter by hand to make sure everything is incorporated. Add the batter to your cake pans. Evenly distribute the cake batter between the pans and fill until they are 1/2 to 3/4 of the way full.

17. If you are using cake strips, put those around the cake pans before putting them in the oven.

18. Baking time will vary depending on the cake size and thickness. I like to set a timer for about 35 minutes to check on how the cake is doing. I will then bake for additional time as necessary. The cake is done when a toothpick comes out clean and the sides start to pull away from the edge of the pan.

19. Take the cake out of the oven and let it cool in the pans for about 15 minutes.

20. Remove the cake from the pans and let it completely cool on a cooling rack.

21. Either frost the cake or store it in an airtight container. The cake will last for about 1 day at room temperature, or 7 days in the refrigerator. You can freeze the cake layers in plastic wrap for up to 2 weeks if you want to make them ahead of time. You could also freeze any leftover cake that has been frosted for up to 3 months in an airtight container.

PECAN CAKE

Ingredients

	Sea Level	3,000 ft	5,000 ft	7,500 ft	10,000 ft
Oven Temp	350 °F	350 °F	360 °F	360 °F	360 °F
Eggs (large)	4	4	5	5	5
Milk	1 cup				
Buttermilk		1 cup	1 cup plus 2 tbsp	1 1/4 cup	1 1/3 cup
Butter	1 cup	1 cup	1 cup	1 cup	1 cup
Granulated Sugar	1 2/3 cups	1 2/3 cups minus 1 tbsp	1 2/3 cups minus 2 tbsp	1 2/3 cups minus 2 tbsp	1 2/3 cups minus 2 tbsp
Brown Sugar	1/3 cup	1/3 cup	1/3 cup	1/3 cup	1/3 cup
All-Purpose Flour	2 2/3 cups	2 2/3 cups	2 2/3 cups plus 3 tbsp	2 2/3 cups plus 3 tbsp	2 2/3 cups plus 3 tbsp
Pecans (finely ground)	1/3 cup	1/3 cup	1/3 cup	1/3 cup	1/3 cup
Salt	3/4 tsp	3/4 tsp	1 tsp	1 tsp	1 tsp
Baking Powder	1 tbsp	2 1/2 tsp	2 tsp	1 1/2 tsp	1 tsp
Vanilla Extract	1 1/2 tsp	1 1/2 tsp	1 1/2 tsp	1 1/2 tsp	1 1/2 tsp

Instructions

1. Preheat your oven according to the temperature in the chart above.
2. If you are using cake strips, place them in a small bowl of water to soak.
3. Crack your eggs into a small bowl and set aside.
4. Measure out your milk or buttermilk and set aside.

5. Prepare your baking pans. Use 1-2 tsp of avocado oil (or your oil of choice) to grease your pans. Then use 2-3 tbsp of flour to dust your pans.

6. Cut parchment paper to fit in the bottom of your pans and place it in the bottom.

7. Using a food processor or another method, grind your pecans into a fine powder.

8. In a small bowl combine the flour, ground pecans, salt and baking powder. Mix with a fork until they are incorporated.

9. Add the butter, granulated sugar and brown sugar to your mixing bowl. Mix on medium high to high speed for a few minutes, until the mixture starts to get fluffy. Scrape the bowl and mix for another 30 seconds.

10. Add in half of the eggs and mix until just combined. Add in the rest of the eggs and mix until just combined.

11. Scrape the bowl and add in the vanilla extract. Mix until combined.

12. Add in half of the milk or buttermilk and mix until combined.

13. Add in half of the flour mixture and mix until combined.

14. Add in the rest of the milk or buttermilk and mix until combined

15. Add in the rest of the flour mixture and mix until combined.

16. Mix the batter by hand to make sure everything is incorporated. Add the batter to your cake pans. Evenly distribute the cake batter between the pans and fill until they are 1/2 to 3/4 of the way full.

17. If you are using cake strips, put those around the cake pans before putting them in the oven.

18. Baking time will vary depending on the cake size and thickness. I like to set a timer for about 35 minutes to check on how the cake is doing. I will then bake for additional time as necessary. The cake is done when a toothpick comes out clean and the sides start to pull away from the edge of the pan.

19. Take the cake out of the oven and let it cool in the pans for about 15 minutes.

20. Remove the cake from the pans and let it completely cool on a cooling rack.

21. Either frost the cake or store it in an airtight container. The cake will last for about 1 day at room temperature, or 7 days in the refrigerator. You can freeze the cake layers in plastic wrap for up to 2 weeks if you want to make them ahead of time. You could also freeze any leftover cake that has been frosted for up to 3 months in an airtight container.

PISTACHIO CAKE

Ingredients

	Sea Level	3,000 ft	5,000 ft	7,500 ft	10,000 ft
Oven Temp	350 °F	350 °F	360 °F	360 °F	360 °F
Eggs (large)	4	4	5	5	5
Milk	1 cup				
Buttermilk		1 cup	1 cup plus 2 tbsp	1 1/4 cup	1 1/3 cup
Butter	1 cup	1 cup	1 cup	1 cup	1 cup
Granulated Sugar	2 cups	2 cups minus 1 tbsp	2 cups minus 2 tbsp	2 cups minus 2 tbsp	2 cups minus 2 tbsp
All-Purpose Flour	2 2/3 cups	2 2/3 cups	2 2/3 cups plus 3 tbsp	2 2/3 cups plus 3 tbsp	2 2/3 cups plus 3 tbsp
Salted Pistachios (finely ground)	1/3 cup	1/3 cup	1/3 cup	1/3 cup	1/3 cup
Salt	1/4 tsp	1/4 tsp	1/4 tsp	1/4 tsp	1/4 tsp
Baking Powder	1 tbsp	2 1/2 tsp	2 tsp	1 1/2 tsp	1 tsp
Vanilla Extract	1 1/2 tsp	1 1/2 tsp	1 1/2 tsp	1 1/2 tsp	1 1/2 tsp

Instructions

1. Preheat your oven according to the temperature in the chart above.
2. If you are using cake strips, place them in a small bowl of water to soak.
3. Crack your eggs into a small bowl and set aside.
4. Measure out your milk or buttermilk and set aside.

MOUNTAINSIDE
Bakery

5. Prepare your baking pans. Use 1-2 tsp of avocado oil (or your oil of choice) to grease your pans. Then use 2-3 tbsp of flour to dust your pans.

6. Cut parchment paper to fit in the bottom of your pans and place it in the bottom.

7. Using a food processor or another method, grind your pistachios into a fine powder. I used salted pistachios, if you use unsalted pistachios then use 1 tsp salt instead.

8. In a small bowl combine the flour, ground pistachios, salt and baking powder. Mix with a fork until they are incorporated.

9. Add the butter and sugar to your mixing bowl. Mix on medium high to high speed for a few minutes, until the mixture starts to get fluffy. Scrape the bowl and mix for another 30 seconds.

10. Add in half of the eggs and mix until just combined. Add in the rest of the eggs and mix until just combined.

11. Scrape the bowl and add in the vanilla extract. Mix until combined.

12. Add in half of the milk or buttermilk and mix until combined.

13. Add in half of the flour mixture and mix until combined.

14. Add in the rest of the milk or buttermilk and mix until combined

15. Add in the rest of the flour mixture and mix until combined.

16. Mix the batter by hand to make sure everything is incorporated. Add the batter to your cake pans. Evenly distribute the cake batter between the pans and fill until they are 1/2 to 3/4 of the way full.

17. If you are using cake strips, put those around the cake pans before putting them in the oven.

18. Baking time will vary depending on the cake size and thickness. I like to set a timer for about 35 minutes to check on how the cake is doing. I will then bake for additional time as necessary. The cake is done when a toothpick comes out clean and the sides start to pull away from the edge of the pan.

19. Take the cake out of the oven and let it cool in the pans for about 15 minutes.

20. Remove the cake from the pans and let it completely cool on a cooling rack.

21. Either frost the cake or store it in an airtight container. The cake will last for about 1 day at room temperature, or 7 days in the refrigerator. You can freeze the cake layers in plastic wrap for up to 2 weeks if you want to make them ahead of time. You could also freeze any leftover cake that has been frosted for up to 3 months in an airtight container.

MATCHA CAKE

Ingredients

	Sea Level	3,000 ft	5,000 ft	7,500 ft	10,000 ft
Oven Temp	350 °F	350 °F	360 °F	360 °F	360 °F
Eggs (large)	4	4	5	5	5
Milk	1 cup				
Buttermilk		1 cup	1 cup plus 2 tbsp	1 1/4 cup	1 1/3 cup
Butter	1 cup	1 cup	1 cup	1 cup	1 cup
Granulated Sugar	2 cups	2 cups minus 1 tbsp	2 cups minus 2 tbsp	2 cups minus 2 tbsp	2 cups minus 2 tbsp
All-Purpose Flour	3 cups	3 cups	3 cups plus 3 tbsp	3 cups plus 3 tbsp	3 cups plus 3 tbsp
Salt	3/4 tsp	3/4 tsp	1 tsp	1 tsp	1 tsp
Baking Powder	1 tbsp	2 1/2 tsp	2 tsp	1 1/2 tsp	1 tsp
Matcha Powder	3 tbsp	3 tbsp	3 tbsp	3 tbsp	3 tbsp
Vanilla Extract	2 tsp	2 tsp	2 tsp	2 tsp	2 tsp

Instructions

1. Preheat your oven according to the temperature in the chart above.
2. If you are using cake strips, place them in a small bowl of water to soak.
3. Crack your eggs into a small bowl and set aside.
4. Measure out your milk or buttermilk and set aside.
5. Prepare your baking pans. Use 1-2 tsp of avocado oil (or your oil of choice) to grease your pans. Then use 2-3 tbsp of flour to dust your pans.

6. Cut parchment paper to fit in the bottom of your pans and place it in the bottom.

7. In a small bowl combine the flour, salt, baking powder and matcha powder. Mix with a fork until they are incorporated.

8. Add the butter and sugar to your mixing bowl. Mix on medium high to high speed for a few minutes, until the mixture starts to get fluffy. Scrape the bowl and mix for another 30 seconds.

9. Add in half of the eggs and mix until just combined. Add in the rest of the eggs and mix until just combined.

10. Scrape the bowl and add in the vanilla extract. Mix until combined.

11. Add in half of the milk or buttermilk and mix until combined.

12. Add in half of the flour mixture and mix until combined.

13. Add in the rest of the milk or buttermilk and mix until combined

14. Add in the rest of the flour mixture and mix until combined.

15. Mix the batter by hand to make sure everything is incorporated. Add the batter to your cake pans. Evenly distribute the cake batter between the pans and fill until they are 1/2 to 3/4 of the way full.

16. If you are using cake strips, put those around the cake pans before putting them in the oven.

17. Baking time will vary depending on the cake size and thickness. I like to set a timer for about 35 minutes to check on how the cake is doing. I will then bake for additional time as necessary. The cake is done when a toothpick comes out clean and the sides start to pull away from the edge of the pan.

18. Take the cake out of the oven and let it cool in the pans for about 15 minutes.

19. Remove the cake from the pans and let it completely cool on a cooling rack.

20. Either frost the cake or store it in an airtight container. The cake will last for about 1 day at room temperature, or 7 days in the refrigerator. You can freeze the cake layers in plastic wrap for up to 2 weeks if you want to make them ahead of time. You could also freeze any leftover cake that has been frosted for up to 3 months in an airtight container.

Frosting Recipes

FROSTING GUIDE

How much frosting will the recipe make?

Each of these recipes will make enough frosting to cover the following cakes and cupcakes with some leftover to decorate:

- 24 dozen cupcakes
- 2 layer 6 inch cake
- 2 layer 8 inch cake

Frosting Tips

1. If your butter gets too soft, place it back into the fridge. If you are in a time crunch then just use another stick of butter and soften it less than the first one.

2. Try to frost your cakes below 72 degrees if possible. The frosting will get soft very quickly and will be hard to work with if it is over 72 degrees. If it is hotter than that, try to frost quickly or make sure your cake is frozen before you start.

3. If you are in the middle of frosting and it starts to get too soft, place the frosting in the fridge for a few minutes. You can also place the cake in the fridge or the freezer.

4. Any extra frosting can be kept in the fridge in an airtight container for up to two weeks.

5. You can save frosting in the icing bag, just place it in a container or a plastic bag so it is air tight. If possible remove the metal tip, if not it is fine to leave it on there.

6. If you need to use the icing bag again, leave it out on the counter to warm up. Depending in the temperature it will probably take about 15-20 minutes. I do not recommend putting it in the microwave if it is still in the icing bag. The frosting will not heat evenly and there is a high chance that the outside will begin to melt before the inside is soft. Also you cannot put the metal icing tips in a microwave.

7. Having the right equipment will make frosting a lot easier!

VANILLA FROSTING

Ingredients

- 2 cups butter
- 32 oz. powdered sugar (two 16 oz. bags or about 8 cups)
- 2 tbsp vanilla extract
- 6 tbsp whole milk

Instructions

1. Leave the butter on the counter to soften a bit at room temperature. Or you can place two sticks of butter in the microwave and heat for 9-11 seconds to soften, then repeat with the other two sticks of butter. Once the butter is a little soft but is still firm then it is ready. You should be able to make an indent in the butter if you push firmly.

2. Place the butter in your mixing bowl and beat for a few minutes.

3. Open a bag of powdered sugar and add in about a third of the bag. Mix until combined. Continue until the whole bag is mixed in.

4. Add in the vanilla extract and mix until combined.

5. Open the second bag of powdered sugar and add in about a third of the bag. Mix until combined. Continue until the whole bag is mixed in.

6. Add in 3 tbsp of whole milk. Mix until combined.

7. Add in the last 3 tbsp of milk and mix until combined. If you need to adjust the consistency add in an additional tbsp of milk at a time.

8. Mix the frosting for about 2 minutes. Scrape the bowl, then mix for another minute.

9. Mix the frosting by hand with a spatula or spoonula for a few seconds to try to get out some of the air bubbles and make sure everything is incorporated.

10. Frost your cake, cupcakes, cookies, etc.!

11. Store any leftovers in an airtight container. It will last up to two weeks in the refrigerator, or you could freeze it for up to 3 months.

MOUNTAINSIDE
Bakery

CHOCOLATE FROSTING

Ingredients

- 2 cups butter
- 1 cup cocoa powder
- 32 oz. powdered sugar (two 16 oz. bags or about 8 cups)
- 4 tsp vanilla extract
- 8 tbsp whole milk

Instructions

1. Leave the butter on the counter to soften a bit at room temperature. Or you can place two sticks of butter in the microwave and heat for 9-11 seconds to soften, then repeat with the other two sticks of butter. Once the butter is a little soft but is still firm then it is ready. You should be able to make an indent in the butter if you push firmly.

2. Place the butter in your mixing bowl and beat for a few minutes.

3. Add in your cocoa powder. Mix until combined.

4. Open a bag of powdered sugar and add in about a third of the bag. Mix until combined. Continue until the whole bag is mixed in.

5. Add in the vanilla and mix until combined.

6. Open the second bag of powdered sugar. Add in about a third and mix.

7. Add in 4 tbsp of whole milk. Mix until combined.

8. Add in another third of the powdered sugar and mix. Then add in the last of the powdered sugar and mix until combined.

9. Add in the last 4 tbsp of milk and mix until combined. If you need to adjust the consistency add in a tbsp of milk at a time.

10. Mix the frosting for about 2 minutes. Scrape the bowl, then mix for another minute.

11. Mix the frosting by hand with a spatula or spoonula for a few seconds to try to get out some of the air bubbles and make sure everything is incorporated.

12. Frost your cake, cupcakes, cookies, etc.!

13. Store any leftovers in an airtight container. It will last up to two weeks in the refrigerator, or you could freeze it for up to 3 months

CREAM CHEESE FROSTING

Ingredients

- 1 cup butter
- 16 oz. of cream cheese (two 8 oz. packages)
- 32 oz. powdered sugar (two 16 oz. bags or about 8 cups)
- 2 tsp vanilla extract

Instructions

1. Take out the cream cheese and let it sit on the counter for a few minutes.
2. Leave the butter on the counter to soften a bit at room temperature. Or you can place two sticks of butter in the microwave and heat for 9-11 seconds to soften. Once the butter is a little soft but is still firm then it is ready. You should be able to make an indent in the butter if you push firmly.
3. Place the butter and cream cheese in your mixing bowl and beat for a few minutes.
4. Open a bag of powdered sugar and add in about a third of the bag. Mix until combined. Continue until the whole bag is mixed in.
5. Add in the vanilla extract and mix until combined.
6. Open the second bag of powdered sugar and add in about a third of the bag. Mix until combined. Continue until the whole bag is mixed in.
7. Mix the frosting for about 2 minutes. Scrape the bowl, then mix for another minute.
8. Mix the frosting by hand with a spatula or spoonula for a few seconds to try to get out some of the air bubbles and make sure everything is incorporated.
9. Frost your cake, cupcakes, cookies, etc.!
10. Store any leftovers in an airtight container. It will last up to 10 days in the refrigerator, or you could freeze it for up to 3 months.

MAPLE FROSTING

Ingredients

- 2 cups butter
- 32 oz. powdered sugar (two 16 oz. bags or about 8 cups)
- 2 tsp vanilla extract
- 4 tsp maple syrup
- 2 tbsp whole milk
- 4 tbsp maple syrup

Instructions

1. Leave the butter on the counter to soften a bit at room temperature. Or you can place two sticks of butter in the microwave and heat for 9-11 seconds to soften, then repeat with the other two sticks of butter. Once the butter is a little soft but is still firm then it is ready. You should be able to make an indent in the butter if you push firmly.

2. Place the butter in your mixing bowl and beat for a few minutes.

3. Open a bag of powdered sugar and add in about a third of the bag. Mix until combined. Continue until the whole bag is mixed in.

4. Add in the vanilla extract and 4 tsp of maple syrup. Mix until combined.

5. Open the second bag of powdered sugar and add in about a third of the bag. Mix until combined. Continue until the whole bag is mixed in.

6. Add in 4 tbsp of maple syrup. Mix until combined.

7. Add in 2 tbsp of milk and mix until combined. If you need to adjust the consistency add in an additional tbsp of milk at a time.

8. Mix the frosting for about 2 minutes. Scrape the bowl, then mix for another minute.

9. Mix the frosting by hand with a spatula or spoonula for a few seconds to try to get out some of the air bubbles and make sure everything is incorporated.

10. Frost your cake, cupcakes, cookies, etc.!

11. Store any leftovers in an airtight container. It will last up to two weeks in the refrigerator, or you could freeze it for up to 3 months.

PUMPKIN SPICE FROSTING

Ingredients

- 2 cups butter
- 32 oz. powdered sugar (two 16 oz. bags or about 8 cups)
- 2 tbsp vanilla extract
- 6 tbsp whole milk
- 2 tsp pumpkin spice

Instructions

1. Leave the butter on the counter to soften a bit at room temperature. Or you can place two sticks of butter in the microwave and heat for 9-11 seconds to soften, then repeat with the other two sticks of butter. Once the butter is a little soft but is still firm then it is ready. You should be able to make an indent in the butter if you push firmly.

2. Place the butter in your mixing bowl and beat for a few minutes.

3. Open a bag of powdered sugar and add in about a third of the bag. Mix until combined. Continue until the whole bag is mixed in.

4. Add in the vanilla extract and mix until combined.

5. Open the second bag of powdered sugar and add in about a third of the bag. Mix until combined. Continue until the whole bag is mixed in.

6. Add in 3 tbsp of whole milk. Mix until combined.

7. Add the pumpkin spice and mix until combined.

8. Add in the last 3 tbsp of milk and mix until combined. If you need to adjust the consistency add in an additional tbsp of milk at a time.

9. Mix the frosting for about 2 minutes. Scrape the bowl, then mix for another minute.

10. Mix the frosting by hand with a spatula or spoonula for a few seconds to try to get out some of the air bubbles and make sure everything is incorporated.

11. Frost your cake, cupcakes, cookies, etc.!

12. Store any leftovers in an airtight container. It will last up to two weeks in the refrigerator, or you could freeze it for up to 3 months.

RICOTTA FROSTING

Ingredients

- 1 cup butter
- 1 cup ricotta
- 32 oz. powdered sugar (two 16 oz. bags or about 8 cups)
- 2 tbsp vanilla extract
- 1/8 tsp lemon flavor or extract
- 2 tbsp whole milk

Instructions

1. Leave the butter on the counter to soften a bit at room temperature. Or you can place two sticks of butter in the microwave and heat for 9-11 seconds to soften, then repeat with the other two sticks of butter. Once the butter is a little soft but is still firm then it is ready. You should be able to make an indent in the butter if you push firmly.

2. Place the butter and ricotta cheese in your mixing bowl and beat for a few minutes.

3. Open a bag of powdered sugar and add in about a third of the bag. Mix until combined. Continue until the whole bag is mixed in.

4. Add in the vanilla extract and lemon flavor or extract. Mix until combined.

5. Open the second bag of powdered sugar and add in about a third of the bag. Mix until combined. Continue until the whole bag is mixed in.

6. Add in 3 tbsp of whole milk. Mix until combined.

7. Add in the last 3 tbsp of milk and mix until combined. If you need to adjust the consistency add in an additional tbsp of milk at a time.

8. Mix the frosting for about 2 minutes. Scrape the bowl, then mix for another minute.

9. Mix the frosting by hand with a spatula or spoonula for a few seconds to try to get out some of the air bubbles and make sure everything is incorporated.

10. Frost your cake, cupcakes, cookies, etc.!

11. Store any leftovers in an airtight container. It will last up to two weeks in the refrigerator, or you could freeze it for up to 3 months.

LEMON FROSTING

Ingredients

- 2 cups butter
- 32 oz. powdered sugar (two 16 oz. bags or about 8 cups)
- 2 tsp vanilla extract
- 1 tbsp lemon flavor or extract
- 6 tbsp whole milk

Instructions

1. Leave the butter on the counter to soften a bit at room temperature. Or you can place two sticks of butter in the microwave and heat for 9-11 seconds to soften, then repeat with the other two sticks of butter. Once the butter is a little soft but is still firm then it is ready. You should be able to make an indent in the butter if you push firmly.

2. Place the butter in your mixing bowl and beat for a few minutes.

3. Open a bag of powdered sugar and add in about a third of the bag. Mix until combined. Continue until the whole bag is mixed in.

4. Add in the vanilla extract and lemon flavor or extract. Mix until combined.

5. Open the second bag of powdered sugar and add in about a third of the bag. Mix until combined. Continue until the whole bag is mixed in.

6. Add in 3 tbsp of whole milk. Mix until combined.

7. Add in the last 3 tbsp of milk and mix until combined. If you need to adjust the consistency add in an additional tbsp of milk at a time.

8. Mix the frosting for about 2 minutes. Scrape the bowl, then mix for another minute.

9. Mix the frosting by hand with a spatula or spoonula for a few seconds to try to get out some of the air bubbles and make sure everything is incorporated.

10. Frost your cake, cupcakes, cookies, etc.!

11. Store any leftovers in an airtight container. It will last up to two weeks in the refrigerator, or you could freeze it for up to 3 months.

STRAWBERRY FROSTING

Ingredients

- 2 cups butter
- 32 oz. powdered sugar (two 16 oz. bags or about 8 cups)
- 4 tsp vanilla extract
- 6 tbsp whole milk
- 1/4 cup powdered freeze-dried strawberries

Instructions

1. Leave the butter on the counter to soften a bit at room temperature. Or you can place two sticks of butter in the microwave and heat for 9-11 seconds to soften, then repeat with the other two sticks of butter. Once the butter is a little soft but is still firm then it is ready. You should be able to make an indent in the butter if you push firmly.

2. Place the butter in your mixing bowl and beat for a few minutes.

3. Add about 1 cup of freeze-dried strawberries to your blender and process until it is a powder. Take 1/4 cup of the powder and add it to your butter. Mix until incorporated.

4. Open a bag of powdered sugar and add in about a third of the bag. Mix until combined. Continue until the whole bag is mixed in.

5. Add in the vanilla extract and mix until combined.

6. Open the second bag of powdered sugar and add in about a third of the bag. Mix until combined. Continue until the whole bag is mixed in.

7. Add in 3 tbsp of whole milk. Mix until combined.

8. Add in the last 3 tbsp of milk and mix until combined. If you need to adjust the consistency add in an additional tbsp of milk at a time.

9. Mix the frosting for about 2 minutes. Scrape the bowl, then mix for another minute.

10. Mix the frosting by hand with a spatula or spoonula for a few seconds to try to get out some of the air bubbles and make sure everything is incorporated.

11. Frost your cake, cupcakes, cookies, etc.!

12. Store any leftovers in an airtight container. It will last up to two weeks in the refrigerator, or you could freeze it for up to 3 months.

LAVENDER FROSTING

Ingredients

- 2 cups butter
- 32 oz. powdered sugar (two 16 oz. bags or about 8 cups)
- 2 tsp vanilla extract
- 3 drops lavender essential oil (food grade)
- 6 tbsp whole milk

Instructions

1. Leave the butter on the counter to soften a bit at room temperature. Or you can place two sticks of butter in the microwave and heat for 9-11 seconds to soften, then repeat with the other two sticks of butter. Once the butter is a little soft but is still firm then it is ready. You should be able to make an indent in the butter if you push firmly.

2. Place the butter in your mixing bowl and beat for a few minutes.

3. Open a bag of powdered sugar and add in about a third of the bag. Mix until combined. Continue until the whole bag is mixed in.

4. Add in the vanilla extract and lavender essential oil. Mix until combined.

5. Open the second bag of powdered sugar and add in about a third of the bag. Mix until combined. Continue until the whole bag is mixed in.

6. Add in 3 tbsp of whole milk. Mix until combined.

7. Add in the last 3 tbsp of milk and mix until combined. If you need to adjust the consistency add in an additional tbsp of milk at a time.

8. Mix the frosting for about 2 minutes. Scrape the bowl, then mix for another minute.

9. Mix the frosting by hand with a spatula or spoonula for a few seconds to try to get out some of the air bubbles and make sure everything is incorporated.

10. Frost your cake, cupcakes, cookies, etc.!

11. Store any leftovers in an airtight container. It will last up to two weeks in the refrigerator, or you could freeze it for up to 3 months.

MOUNTAINSIDE
Bakery

ALMOND FROSTING

Ingredients

- 2 cups butter
- 32 oz. powdered sugar (two 16 oz. bags or about 8 cups)
- 1 tsp vanilla extract
- 4 tsp almond extract
- 6 tbsp whole milk

Instructions

1. Leave the butter on the counter to soften a bit at room temperature. Or you can place two sticks of butter in the microwave and heat for 9-11 seconds to soften, then repeat with the other two sticks of butter. Once the butter is a little soft but is still firm then it is ready. You should be able to make an indent in the butter if you push firmly.

2. Place the butter in your mixing bowl and beat for a few minutes.

3. Open a bag of powdered sugar and add in about a third of the bag. Mix until combined. Continue until the whole bag is mixed in.

4. Add in the vanilla and almond extracts. Mix until combined.

5. Open the second bag of powdered sugar and add in about a third of the bag. Mix until combined. Continue until the whole bag is mixed in.

6. Add in 3 tbsp of whole milk. Mix until combined.

7. Add in the last 3 tbsp of milk and mix until combined. If you need to adjust the consistency add in an additional tbsp of milk at a time.

8. Mix the frosting for about 2 minutes. Scrape the bowl, then mix for another minute.

9. Mix the frosting by hand with a spatula or spoonula for a few seconds to try to get out some of the air bubbles and make sure everything is incorporated.

10. Frost your cake, cupcakes, cookies, etc.!

11. Store any leftovers in an airtight container. It will last up to two weeks in the refrigerator, or you could freeze it for up to 3 months.

CHOCOLATE ORANGE FROSTING

Ingredients

- 2 cups butter
- 1 cup cocoa powder
- 32 oz. powdered sugar (two 16 oz. bags or about 8 cups)
- 4 tsp vanilla extract
- 1/2 tsp orange flavor or extract
- 8 tbsp whole milk

Instructions

1. Leave the butter on the counter to soften a bit at room temperature. Or you can place two sticks of butter in the microwave and heat for 9-11 seconds to soften, then repeat with the other two sticks of butter. Once the butter is a little soft but is still firm then it is ready. You should be able to make an indent in the butter if you push firmly.

2. Place the butter in your mixing bowl and beat for a few minutes.

3. Add in your cocoa powder. Mix until combined.

4. Open a bag of powdered sugar and add in about a third of the bag. Mix until combined. Continue until the whole bag is mixed in.

5. Add in the vanilla extract and orange flavor. Mix until combined.

6. Open the second bag of powdered sugar. Add in about a third and mix.

7. Add in 4 tbsp of whole milk. Mix until combined.

8. Add in another third of the powdered sugar and mix. Then add in the last of the powdered sugar and mix until combined.

9. Add in the last 4 tbsp of milk and mix until combined. If you need to adjust the consistency add in a tbsp of milk at a time.

10. Mix the frosting for about 2 minutes. Scrape the bowl, then mix for another minute.

11. Mix the frosting by hand with a spatula or spoonula for a few seconds to try to get out some of the air bubbles and make sure everything is incorporated.

12. Frost your cake, cupcakes, cookies, etc.!

13. Store any leftovers in an airtight container. It will last up to two weeks in the refrigerator, or you could freeze it for up to 3 months.

MOUNTAINSIDE
Bakery

PEPPERMINT FROSTING

Ingredients

- 2 cups butter
- 32 oz. powdered sugar (two 16 oz. bags or about 8 cups)
- 4 tsp vanilla extract
- 1 tsp peppermint extract
- 6 tbsp whole milk

Instructions

1. Leave the butter on the counter to soften a bit at room temperature. Or you can place two sticks of butter in the microwave and heat for 9-11 seconds to soften, then repeat with the other two sticks of butter. Once the butter is a little soft but is still firm then it is ready. You should be able to make an indent in the butter if you push firmly.

2. Place the butter in your mixing bowl and beat for a few minutes.

3. Open a bag of powdered sugar and add in about a third of the bag. Mix until combined. Continue until the whole bag is mixed in.

4. Add in the vanilla and peppermint extracts. Mix until combined.

5. Open the second bag of powdered sugar and add in about a third of the bag. Mix until combined. Continue until the whole bag is mixed in.

6. Add in 3 tbsp of whole milk. Mix until combined.

7. Add in the last 3 tbsp of milk and mix until combined. If you need to adjust the consistency add in an additional tbsp of milk at a time.

8. Mix the frosting for about 2 minutes. Scrape the bowl, then mix for another minute.

9. Mix the frosting by hand with a spatula or spoonula for a few seconds to try to get out some of the air bubbles and make sure everything is incorporated.

10. Frost your cake, cupcakes, cookies, etc.!

11. Store any leftovers in an airtight container. It will last up to two weeks in the refrigerator, or you could freeze it for up to 3 months.

IRISH CREAM FROSTING

Ingredients

- 2 cups butter
- 32 oz. powdered sugar (two 16 oz. bags or about 8 cups)
- 4 tsp vanilla extract
- 6 tbsp Irish Cream

Instructions

1. Leave the butter on the counter to soften a bit at room temperature. Or you can place two sticks of butter in the microwave and heat for 9-11 seconds to soften, then repeat with the other two sticks of butter. Once the butter is a little soft but is still firm then it is ready. You should be able to make an indent in the butter if you push firmly.

2. Place the butter in your mixing bowl and beat for a few minutes.

3. Open a bag of powdered sugar and add in about a third of the bag. Mix until combined. Continue until the whole bag is mixed in.

4. Add in the vanilla extract and mix until combined.

5. Open the second bag of powdered sugar and add in about a third of the bag. Mix until combined. Continue until the whole bag is mixed in.

6. Add in 3 tbsp of Irish Cream. Mix until combined.

7. Add in the last 3 tbsp of Irish Cream and mix until combined. If you need to adjust the consistency add in an additional tbsp of milk at a time.

8. Mix the frosting for about 2 minutes. Scrape the bowl, then mix for another minute.

9. Mix the frosting by hand with a spatula or spoonula for a few seconds to try to get out some of the air bubbles and make sure everything is incorporated.

10. Frost your cake, cupcakes, cookies, etc.!

11. Store any leftovers in an airtight container. It will last up to two weeks in the refrigerator, or you could freeze it for up to 3 months.

Thank you so much for purchasing my recipe book! I hope it helps you successfully bake a cake! Follow me for more recipes and tips!

https://mountainsidebakery.com/
@mtnsidebakery

Made in the USA
Columbia, SC
21 April 2023

d3dd2d39-bc35-4a3f-acec-8d42ad90c8c3R01